A Man called Jones
and his Smallest House

Margaret Williams

*My thanks to the family of Robert Jones, especially Mary Jones,
Liz Jordan, Betty Jones-Williams, Megan Jones and
John Hughes, to William Craven-Davies and to the staff
at Llandudno reference library*

*Cover picture by Philip Micheu-De-Dubois from a portrait
in oils circa 1900*

ISBN: 0-86381-382-8

*First published in 1996 by Gwasg Carreg Gwalch,
Llanrwst, Wales.*

Tel: 01492 642031

Printed in Wales.

For Joshua Jefferies who wanted to know more about his great great great grandfather

The Gentlemen of Conwy

They met that evening as they always did, in the bar parlour of the Black Lion, the inn on Conwy's Castle Street which used to be the residence of Vicar John Bricknall whose initials, along with those of his wife and the date 1589 are still over the front door.

But this was not in the golden days of Queen Elizabeth. The year was 1900, the start of what everyone hoped would be an exciting new century, especially here in North Wales which was being discovered by visitors from over the border now that the railway line had been built along the coast.

Before this it had been the exclusive retreat of a number of well known people, including Mr Gladstone who had visited Penmaenmawr for 40 years. A memorial to him had been erected there, something that was attracting the attention of the early tourists and now everyone was looking forward to the day when Queen Victoria was due to travel by train from Holyhead to Windsor on her way from Ireland, many hoping to catch a glimpse of her at Llandudno Junction station, and also to the visit of Madame Patti who was to sing at Colwyn Bay that summer.

Here they were, the gentlemen of Conwy, something they were proud of being called. For many years before this, the saying 'the lawyers of Caernarfon, the merchants of Beaumaris and the *gentlemen* of Conwy' had come about when Caernarfon became the administrative centre for North Wales and Beaumaris the trading port. Now, in the Black Lion, the gentlemen of the town sat with their drinks overlooking the yard where there was a pig market every Monday morning while the street outside was the scene of nine fairs every year, dating back to the time when Edward I of England, who had created a town here, allowed the Welsh to trade within the walls on one day every week.

The doctor, the lawyer, the cabinet maker, the shipowner, the editor of the local newspaper and the captain home from the sea were all here, but one of the company was missing.

'Robert's late tonight,' the doctor observed.

'He's had some bad news,' said the editor of the *North Wales Weekly News*, Mr Roger Dawson. 'Some of his property on the quayside is to be demolished.'

'So?'

'A few of the houses are apparently too small for people to live in and he's been told to find somewhere else for his tenants so he's very preoccupied.'

'We'll hear all about it when he comes,' said the lawyer.

'No doubt,' commented the editor, changing the subject to events of the day, for Conwy had set up its own Transvaal War Relief Fund and his paper was appealing for socks and pocket handkerchiefs for the men of the Royal Welch Fusiliers serving in South Africa.

But when Robert Jones entered the room he did not wish to discuss Kruger and the Cape Colony or the latest on Free Trade. His mind was on his property.

'All the small houses must go, that's what the man from the Corporation told me' he said. 'The others, from my own house along the row, are all right, thank goodness. But this is a nuisance, it's going to cause me a lot of trouble and bother.'

'That one next to yours, why is it so small?' the editor asked curiously.

'When they built the houses they started at either end, met in the middle with a space and then filled it in. They only needed a front wall and a roof and chimney, the back wall is actually part of a tower of the town walls!'

They all laughed, but Robert Jones was sombre. 'This is not very funny — '

'Wait a minute,' said the editor. 'How big is that house?'

'Seventy two inches across, 122 inches high and 120 inches in depth, that's what the fellow from the Corporation said after he'd measured it.'

A gleam came into the editor's eye. 'I've just thought of something — ' he began.

'Then let it wait a few minutes, it's time we were on the move,' said the lawyer. They walked out of the Black Lion, crossed the road and went up High Street to the Castle Hotel where, in the bar reserved exclusively for gentlemen, the editor told them what had been going through his mind.

'That tiny house could well be the smallest in the British Isles.'

The fishing tradition

Robert Jones was clearly a man ahead of his time and many said he inherited his powerful personality from his mother. Determined to be the first person to walk across Telford's newly-built suspension bridge which replaced the centuries-old ferry in 1826 she defied warnings and orders and sauntered forth triumphantly to the cries of protest all around her, her cloak billowing and the streamers of her bonnet fluttering in the breeze.

Well-built and with a generous white beard, Robert Jones lived in a 16th century house on the quayside where a parrot in a cage suspended from one of the oak beams squawked colourful expletives whenever anyone crossed the threshold — in Welsh, of course! From here Robert Jones ran a prosperous fishing industry, employing men and about 40 women who rowed to the mussel beds throughout the winter gathering the blue shellfish which were then sent to the markets of England.

The mussels are indeed part of Conwy's history for when the Cistercian monks established their abbey here in 1186 they taught the upland dwellers how to farm their lands and those living by the river the art of fishing. It was the monks who invented the long-handled rakes topped with net which are upturned to gather the mussels, the method used to this day.

Sometimes pearls were found in mussel shells and an exceptionally large one is in the Crown Jewels, having been presented to Catherine, the consort of Charles II by her chamberlain, Sir Richard Wynne of Gwydir. This particular pearl came from the mussel known as the *Mya Margaritifera* (Cragen y Dilyw), gathered in the higher part of the river beyond Trefriw.

Pearl fishing is said to date back to the Roman conquest. Julius Caesar dedicated a breastplate to Venus Genitrix, covered with British pearls, which was placed in her temple in Rome. So it is possible that the site of the Roman camp at Caer Rhun, a few miles from Conwy, was chosen because of its proximity to the mussel beds.

The pearl industry flourished over the years. During its heyday there was a pearl kitchen on the Morfa, a small building of wattle and gorse with a hole in the roof for the smoke to escape, and here the mussels were boiled in a large iron pot then picked out and put into a tub and crushed by bare-footed children jumping on them. The pearls were put into little bags and taken to be sold in Chester, usually for between six and twelve shillings an ounce.

In 1838 the Blue Book containing the reports of Municipal Corporations stated 'They pay £1 a year for the land where they boil the mussels.' Around that time there were 40 people employed in the fishery which produced an average of about 160 ounce of pearls a week, said to be equal to any found in Britain.

Mussels became a highly desirable delicacy and the merchants of Manchester were quick to respond to the demand of the discerning, walking all the way to Conwy to negotiate with people like Robert Jones, often wearing out a pair of clogs on their long trek.

The mussel season ended in April after which the gatherers laid down their rakes and took up finely meshed nets to fish for the sparling, tiny fish with transparent heads and skin so thin the blood can be seen circulating. These spawn in March or April and have their own distinctive smell, compared by some to cucumber but more properly to rushes — hence their Welsh name *brwyniad*.

Legend has it that once, when there was a great famine in the land and not even enough fish to allay the hunger of the people, Saint Ffraid gathered a quantity of rushes which she threw into the river, and on hitting the water they immediately changed into fully grown fish.

When the sparlings left, the fishers would go up river to Tal-y-cafn where they dragged their nets for salmon in the upper reaches.

The boats of these men and women were not the only craft in the river for Conwy was a busy port with foundries on the banks and sloops and schooners a familiar sight. Copper was shipped from the Great Orme mines to Swansea; from Conwy went wheat to Ireland, oatmeal to Scotland, oats, wheat, barley, beans and peas to Liverpool, and the ash of seaweed burned for potash which was used in the soap works of Warrington.

Slate was brought from the upland quarries to Trefriw by cart, thence to Conwy in sailing boats where it was transferred to larger vessels. Coal, groceries, earthenware and salt were imported while three-masted ships from the Baltic unloaded timber at the mouth of the Gyffin stream for the sawmills there.

The decline of the port

Robert Jones saw the decline of the port when the railway was built along the coastline but this iron way opened North Wales to the first tourists and soon large hotels were being built in the new resorts of Llandudno and Colwyn Bay with guests anxious to taste the fruits of the sea as well as bathe in it. Robert Jones was now selling his mussels and fish to these hotels as well as to the Manchester and Sheffield markets and soon word of this spread south and it was not long before he was sending a bag of mussels every week by train to a famous West End restaurant.

A casual observer of the time would have thought it strange that while Robert Jones's biggest boat was called the *Mari Fach*, two of the others bore the names of English politicians — Disraeli (later to be changed to Lord Beaconsfield on the politician's elevation to the peerage!) and Lord Salisbury. This was because he was determined to show his political allegiance as this was the constituency of young Liberal solicitor David Lloyd George who had won the election by a majority of just 18 but whose popularity was soaring rapidly.

It was from one of these boats that Robert Jones and his brother netted a sturgeon which he proudly displayed on the beach near his home until the police bore down on him with a reminder that he had not offered it to its rightful owner. For since the reign of Edward II, the first English Prince of Wales, all sturgeon caught off the coasts of Britain, except in certain privileged places, have belonged to the Sovereign. When the Palace declined to accept, the sturgeon was bought by the Royal Fish Stores in Llandudno — so called because Queen Marie of Roumania had patronised it on her visit to this, the queen of the Welsh resorts.

The sturgeon — the last to be caught in Conwy — was not Robert Jones's family's only 'first'. With his brother and one of his sons he netted a 65 lb salmon at Tal-y-cafn while his grandson Jack and nephew John Hugh caught a 50 lb one in the same spot many years later.

Family Roots

Robert Jones's family roots went back into the mists of time.

When Edward I built his town here he did not allow the Welsh to live within the walls. This rule was only relaxed in Tudor times and the first house to be built by a Welshman was the magnificent Plas Mawr in the High Street, the home of Elizabethan adventurer Robert Wynne of Gwydir. One of Robert Jones's ancestors built a row of houses on the quayside, but as he explained to his friends, building work started at either end, resulting in a space in the centre which was soon filled in with a wall and a roof and became a tiny dwelling comprising but two rooms linked by a wooden stairway.

People lived in the house down the years. They cooked on the fire in the tiny grate, sat on a wooden settle under which the coal was stored and washed with water from a tap behind the stairs. An elderly married couple slept on a double mattress placed on the floor — they had to roll the mattress up before they could open the trap door and let themselves out of the bedroom.

When they left the house a fisherman also called Robert Jones lived there for 15 years — he must have been most uncomfortable for he was six feet three inches tall! And when the Corporation officials came to inspect the premises he said to them 'I think I had better step outside so that you can come in!'

Roger Dawson, the editor of the local paper, was acutely conscious that North Wales would soon be a Mecca for tourists from the North of England and because of this he urged in his columns that more money should be spent on the resorts to make them more pleasant places for visitors. He was convinced that this house could well be the smallest in the land and would therefore be an asset to Conwy. So he sent a story to all the daily newspapers stating Conwy's claim. Back came the replies he wanted — people in a number of towns and villages wrote in to say there was an equally tiny dwelling where they lived. This way he found out where all the other small houses were and he then insisted that he and Robert Jones visit them to prove his point.

Together they went to Ambleside, the Bayswater Road in London, Devon and Cornwall and established that the house at Conwy was smaller than any they had seen.

Now that visitors were coming to the North Wales coast there was renewed interest in the castle, while the two oldest houses, Aberconwy and Plas Mawr, were also opened to the public.

So the small house on the quay joined the ranks of the great mansions and people came to marvel at the compact interior where a way of life had gone on for centuries. At first, there was no admission charge, people just left a donation but then it was decided to ask for one penny, subsequently to be increased to twopence, a price that remained until decimilisation.

Soon visitors were asking could they buy postcards so Robert Jones had two pictures taken — one of his second wife, Jane, dressed in Welsh costume, knitting by the front door, the other of the last tenant standing outside. Both these cards are still sold to the public.

Robert Jones had hit on something unique but at first it was not all plain sailing. His two sons, William and John, were not keen on the idea and said so but their father heeded not for he cared little for the opinions of others, proving this when he stood up in church and opposed the banns of his daughter because she was under age — the last person ever to do so at Saint Mary's.

His children were by his first wife Elizabeth, whom he married at St Mary's Church on Christmas Day, 1861, a woman who is still talked about in Conwy because of the part she played in the early days of one particular section of the community.

On a summer morning a strange boat with just one man on board dropped anchor in the middle of the river. He was known to some as James Craven, from Blackpool who, along with other fishermen of the Fylde coast came to North Wales whenever fish petered out in Morecambe Bay. They based themselves at Llanddulas, moving to Conwy, Caernarfon and Pwllheli but they always returned to Blackpool.

But this time James Craven intended to stay, his interest being a local girl, Ellen Jones, whom he had met briefly and wanted to see again.

The Conwy fishermen refused to let him land, reckoning that he would depart for England as soon as his food supplies ran out.

He astounded them all by staying and Robert Jones's wife aided the course of true love by rowing herself out with a hot meal for him, despite the outcry all around her that in doing this she was encouraging foreigners to fish the waters.

She knew the right time to go to the aid of the Englishman, when Robert Jones was safely out of the way, for on this particular day he had gone to Tal-y-cafn, four miles up river, to fetch a Welsh dresser which Conwy solicitor and Clerk to the Justices James Porter had bought at a house sale. Bringing this to Conwy had presented difficulties for the lanes from Tal-y-cafn were narrow and twisted and there was a danger of the dresser being damaged. Then Robert Jones decided to tie it with ropes to the stern of a stout boat which he would row down river.

When he said what he was going to do, everyone thought he was mad, arguing that nobody could pull at oars with a great weight like that in the boat for such a distance. But he laughed, as he always did when meeting a challenge, for he hated to think that anything could defeat him.

So down river he went on that beautiful morning with his precious load tied securely to the stern of his boat. But as he completed the final lap to the shore at Conwy he met a strange sight — his wife surrounded by excited, angry men and women. He was soon to know what had happened.

*   *   *

James Craven eventually married Ellen Jones and they had seven sons and a daughter who went on to start what is now one of the largest families in the town.

After what was indeed a spectacular life, Robert Jones died in 1915. His parrot died three days later, many said from grief.

Robert Jones left the house to his second wife Jane for the remainder of her days — he lists this marriage under Other

Events in the family Bible! He by-passed his sons, the house being subsequently left to his grand-daughter Elizabeth, daughter of his son John. Elizabeth married Robert Williams, the scion of an equally old family who had lived in Plas Mawr and then moved to the neighbouring Old Mansion House. During her ownership the house gained a place in the *Guinness Book of Records*. On her death in 1987 the Smallest House became the property of their daughter Margaret, the writer of this booklet.

During recent years the number of visitors from overseas has increased tremendously and because of this there is now a recorded commentary in 15 languages.

Now that the house has become so well known, Margaret Williams finds she is being asked to give talks on its history to groups and societies in this country and abroad and she has lectured to American tourists travelling to our shores on board the liner *Queen Elizabeth II*, something she feels Robert Jones would have approved of in view of his strong links with the sea. She and her helpers dress in Welsh costume as his second wife did when she posed for the postcard picture all those years ago.

These days, when most people enjoy a good standard of living, the Smallest House is more of a curiosity than it ever was for few can visualise the way of life that was normal until the turn of the century when one was considered fortunate to have the mere basics and when even the thought of luxuries was beyond the imagination of a community that wrested its livelihood from the sea.

The gentlemen of Conwy.

Robert Jones, son William and Togo pose for an early photographer recording the industries of North Wales.

Robert Jones outside the Smallest House with his dog Togo.

The family boats sailing off Deganwy.

Trading vessels tied up at the quay in winter.

*The sturgeon beached. Looking on is former mayor
Dr R. Arthur-Prichard JP.*

Robert Jones and some of his mussel gatherers.

Fishing boats in the shadow of the castle.

The fishing fleet in harbour.

The castle and quay in the last century.

Margaret Williams chatting to visitors outside the house.

The Smallest House in 1900 shortly after it had been opened to the public as a showplace. The two cottages on the left were part of the row that was demolished shortly after this picture was taken.

The last tenant, also called Robert Jones, standing outside the Smallest House.

The owner's wife Jane, dressed in traditional Welsh costume, posed for this 1900 postcard, copies of which are still selling to visitors.

Robert Jones's great grandson Brian Jones outside the house with a mussel rake, the like of which has been used since the 12th century. To the right is the interior of the house, the tiny living room and bedroom.

Also by the same author:

The Smallest House Cook Book
£1.95